A ROYAL DISGRACE:

I FELL NOW WHAT?

FINDING RESTORATION OF SONSHIP IN THE KINGDOM OF GOD

DWAYNE JACOBS

3 TREES

3 TREES
PUBLISHING

3Trees Publishing
18024 Dedeaux Clan
Gulfport, MS

DEDICATION

I dedicate this book first of all to prodigals around the globe, as a call to return to the Father who loves you more than you can comprehend. For God so loved the world, he gave his only begotten son that whosoever believeth in him should not perish, but have everlasting life. God sent not his son into the world to condemn the world: but that the world through him might be saved. John 3:16-17

Secondly I dedicate this book to my beautiful wife who is, and always has been, an inspiration to me. She has been instrumental in helping me realize and understand that it is the love of God that draws men to repentance. When I felt like I had messed up so bad; that I was done with ministry; her prophetic voice, through love, helped me break away from religion and taught me much about the Fathers love, and having a relationship with the Father.

Next, to my three sons: Jonathan, Brandon and Holden as well as my four daughters: Victoria, Olivia, Cayla and Tabby - for the life lessons I have learned through raising them and discovering the depth of the Fathers love, because of the love I have for them. A love that goes deeper than words, not based on how well they perform their duties; but a love in action that is expressed through the good times and the bad times. They have helped me realize how much the Father loves us even when we did not love Him. The Bible says in Romans 5:8:

> *But God demonstrates his own love for us in this: while we were still sinners Christ died for us.*

This is a love that is unconditional.

CONTENTS

INTRODUCTION

This book was birthed after experiencing a time of feeling alienated from Father God. I had walked away from Father, and the farther I went, the more alienated I felt. There are many things one ponders when you have sinned against God, and hit rock bottom after walking with Him, having moved in His anointing, then being tripped up by the enemy. Thoughts arise that say that 'you're not good enough,' 'look at what you have done,' 'you're so unworthy,' ... I could go on and on.

When I came to my senses and realized life is so much better in the Father's house, it was time to go home. Upon making this decision I was met with multiple challenges. Would I be accepted? Would I be welcomed back into the kingdom? Would God be willing to trust me with the gifting He originally gave me? The answer is yes, a hundred times over. I finally came to the decision: "I just want to be with God in heaven when my time here on earth is done." As Holy Spirit pursued me, I surrendered and received Fathers glorious forgiveness, and was restored instantly into the kingdom.

God said, "I want you to write a book entitled: *I Fell Now What?*" God told me, "I have many Generals that have fallen into the trap of the enemy and have just given up. It is My desire to restore My people. I miss My time with those whom I have called to do My work." He said, "I want you to call the prodigals home."

My prayer is that anyone reading this book will see the Father's heart and love for His kids. May you lay aside every weight and sin that would so easily trip you up. Realize you are loved by Father! He has never stopped loving you. You are a peculiar people, a chosen generation a royal priesthood, a holy nation that should show forth praises of him who has called you out of darkness into his marvelous light.

The pigpen is no place for the believer! Come to the Father! He is waiting for you with open arms. He longs to have true intimacy with you. Father is waiting to exchange your soiled garments for a robe of righteousness.

When the prodigal son began the journey home, he had one thought in mind: to be reunited with his father. Whatever it looked like and whatever happened, he knew he would be in better shape in the father's house. Even as a servant, his life would be better than the pigpen!

Amazingly when the father saw his son afar off, he ran to him and kissed him. He didn't scorn him for smelling like the pigpen. He didn't say, "Come quickly, let's burn your clothes, get a scrub brush and give you a bath!" No! He put a robe on his son! He placed a ring on his finger, shoes on his feet, and threw him a party!

Do you remember when you first came to Father? Did you feel the weight of sin lift off your life? Did you experience the freedom in Christ when you accepted Him as Lord and Savior? If so, He wants to restore all of that right now! He is ready, willing, and able. If you have never experienced what I just described, know that He longs to give it to you: just surrender your life to Him. You were created for Him - allow God to live through you.

> If you will confess with your mouth the Lord Jesus and believe in your heart God has raised him from the dead, you shall be saved. For with the heart one believes unto righteousness, and with the mouth confession is made unto salvation.
>
> ROMANS 10:9-10 (KJV)

> Whoever calls on the name of the Lord shall be saved.
>
> ROMANS 9: 13 (KJV)

Let us arise and be the Kings and Priests God has called us to be. Our gifts and calling are without repentance! Come my brother, my sister! Respond to God and embrace the call upon your life. You can never make enough excuses to take the place of operating in your call. Father sees you where you are. His love for you is unconditional. He loves you!

I have been the one to fall and wallow in my sin - thoughts of faults and failures overwhelmed me. I have walked through the Elder Brother Syndrome and felt the attack of the religious spirit. I know the struggle of dying to self. One day I realized, with the help of my lovely wife, that Father wants us to run into His arms when we fall flat on our face. He will clean us up and make us whole again.

It is my honor to Father to share this with others. May God bless you and bring greater revelation to you as you read through the pages of this book. His robe of righteousness looks good on you! See yourself robed in the righteousness of God.

A ROYAL DISGRACE:

I FELL NOW WHAT?

CHAPTER 1
ARISE AND SHINE

Many mighty men and women called by God have fallen. Some have gotten back up and gone on to do great things in the ministry, with God working with and through them. Others have fallen and let the enemy beat them down to the point of feeling like there is no use to ever try again. Many have asked themselves "Why would God take someone like me back into the ministry?" The devil has convinced others that they have messed up so bad they shouldn't seek forgiveness.

Listen friend, that is the planned attack Satan had against you from the day you accepted Christ! You must remember that you are human just like all the other men God used throughout the Bible - even those that wrote much of the Bible! We have accounts of many that disobeyed God, sinned against Him - even cursed Him - but God was merciful to forgive in His loving mercy.

There was only one human ever lived that was sinless. The religious leaders sought to destroy Him and pressed on until they crucified Him! What they and the devil did not realize is that

He would rise from the dead in three days, and become victorious over death, hell, and the grave!

Wait, there is more! He would give authority to the children of God called by His name to heal the sick, cleanse the lepers, raise the dead and trample the enemy under their feet!

Man and Woman of God: arise and shine for your light has come![1] Your gifts and calling of God are without repentance.[2] Is there breath in your body? Can you ask God to forgive you? Can you believe that He is a rewarder of those that diligently seek him?[3] God is faithful and just to forgive.[4] Jeremiah 1:5 says before you were ever formed in your mother's womb he knew you, chose you and ordained you. Is it not safe to say that God knew you would be where you are, right now, at this very moment? Your fall did not catch God by surprise.

He said of David "The Lord has sought out for Himself a man after His own heart and the Lord has appointed him as leader and ruler over His people."[5] This word was spoken before David became king, so definitely before he committed adultery with Bathsheba and killed Uriah. God knew David had a repentant heart. David's actions may have caught him by surprise, but it did not surprise God.

The enemy wants to convince us that we have messed up too bad to ever be worthy of the blood of Jesus. We are not worthy of the blood. That's why Jesus came and died on the cross to redeem us, because we could never do enough or be good enough to receive the redemption any other way. God loves you right where you are.

If you are reading this book, chances are you want to restore your relationship with your heavenly Father. Simply ask for forgiveness, and accept the fact that God loves you unconditionally. Accept the fact that all have sinned and come short of the glory of God.[6]

Now, forgive yourself. It isn't easy, but you can do it! Holy Spirit will help you. God said, "Ask and it shall be given; seek and you shall find; knock and it shall be opened unto you.[7] Christ died for your sins! Allow His blood to cleanse you, then get up and come to the throne of grace boldly to find help in the time of trouble (need).[8] God never condemned us for falling, however, we condemn ourselves when we just lay there and wallow in our sin! It's not he that starts in the race, but he that endures to the end shall be saved.[9]

Endurance comes through dependence upon God. You may be stuck and feel like you are broken down on the side of the road. You may feel like everyone, even life itself, is passing you by - but cry out to Jesus. He is a caring, loving, and forgiving Father. When we walk with God, He never walks away from us. We sometimes walk away from Him, but He is right where you left Him: waiting and anticipating your return.

The prodigal son is a perfect example. Let's look at the steps he took that led him to desperation. Yes, from desperation back to the father's house where he found his father waiting for him with open arms, anticipating his return. When the son saw his father he said, "I have sinned against heaven, and in your sight and am no more worthy to be called your son." The father did not even acknowledge what the son said. He had no intention of exposing his son's sin and folly, but he commanded a servant to bring the best robe to cover him!

God the Father displays this same type of love to His children. God is not waiting to punish you for falling. He knows you have walked through humiliation, accusation, and slander. He is waiting to lift you up. He wants to bring stability back into your life. He longs to communicate with you to show you His love. In fact, His desire is to turn our mess into a message that others may come know Him. He has great plans for your life: "For I know the plans that I have for you, says the Lord, 'they are plans for good, and not for disaster, to give you a future and a hope.'"[10]

God knows how to give good gifts to his children,[11] and He will not withhold them when the time is right. For instance, I would not give my eight-year-old son the keys to my car and say, "Since this will be yours one day anyway, go ahead and drive to the store and get us some ice cream." Even though it's possible my son could probably drive to the store safely, it would be against the law. God's kingdom is established with laws, and the body functions within the boundaries of Gods law.[12]

Oh the joys of those who do not follow the advice of the wicked or stand around with sinners or join in with mockers! They delight in the law of the Lord, meditating on it day and night.[13]

God commanded us to love our neighbor as we love ourselves,[14] and love the Lord your God with all your heart. He said all the law hangs on these two commands. Let us, therefore, follow God and not become weary in well doing, for in due season we reap, if we faint not.[15]

God has big plans for your future! He has gifts He desires to release to you. We must first get into position to receive those gifts so that we can advance the kingdom and not shipwreck our faith.

God wants to take you higher than you have ever been - will you let go of the reins and let God lead you to higher heights, and deeper depths in Him? Salvation is free bought and paid for by Jesus.

No one knows the cost of the oil in your alabaster box but you, are you willing to pour your oil of praise on Him? Are you ready to return to the Father with a servant's heart?

He is waiting for you to come home.

———————————

1. Isaiah 1:60 KJV
2. Romans 11:29 KJV
3. Hebrews 11:6 KJV
4. 1 John 1:9 KJV
5. 1 Samuel 13:14 KJV
6. Romans 3:23 KJV
7. Matthew 7:7 KJV
8. Hebrews 4:16 KJV
9. Matthew 24:13 KJV
10. Jeremiah 29:11 NLT
11. Matthew 7:9 KJV
12. Psalms 1:1-2 NLT
13. Psalm 1:1-2 TLB
14. Mark 12:31-33 KJV
15. Galatians 6:9 KJV

CHAPTER 2
SELF WILL

The prodigal son was a son in his father's house. Growing up he learned to serve the house in whatever capacity the father authorized. The intent of the father was to groom his son for leadership, or 'headship' as custom would have it.

Not too long after the son felt like he had become a man, he came to the realization that as a son he could ask the father for his inheritance. I believe this young man had a good relationship with his father and felt he could ask for whatever he wanted, and dad would oblige him. So, he asked for his inheritance. The love the father had toward his son was exceptional. Not all fathers would divide and distribute what he was going to leave his kids after his death, so early in life! He divided the inheritance between his sons and gave the younger son his portion.

This is symbolic of what happens when we accept Christ as Lord and Savior of our life: He gives us our inheritance. He gives us eternal life and places gifts on the inside of us. We begin serving in the house of God in whatever capacity that pleases the Father. As we grow in the Lord, our walk deepens, and more responsibility is given unto us.

If we are not careful to keep our guard up, the enemy is very subtle and will plot all sorts of evil against us to tear us down and bring us to destruction. He does not care about you at all - he sees the potential you have as a born-again believer. He is an accuser of the brethren, so he accuses us to ourselves, others, and to God. You must remember he is a liar and the father of lies.

If you make a mistake, bring it to God. Repent, get it under the blood and continue in your walk as a blood bought child of the King. We all have a weakness. No one is exempt from trials and tribulations, but you better know what your weakness is and put distance between yourself and that weakness. I love the way my pastor, Reverend Bryan Matthews say's it, "You better know your kryptonite." God does not need your ability - He needs your availability! We need to make ourselves available for His service, and be ready to do His will.

The enemy, seeking whom he may devour, comes along, and begins to tempt us with the pride of life. Maybe he begins by feeding our ego, and somewhere along the way self-will begins to rise-up within our heart. When we fail to take authority over self-will the flesh begins to rise-up and seek gratification. God never meant for us to be a body with a spirit being led by the flesh. He meant for us to be a body with a spirit, being led by the spirit.

When the flesh has gotten a taste of gratification, selfishness begins to creep in. It does not happen all at once, but a little at a time. The enemy likes to plant seeds of selfishness, envy, and strife in our heart. Through the desires of the flesh, and the pride of life - along with the enticement of the enemy - we are lured away from God.

Once the prodigal son received his portion of inheritance, not long after that, he left the fathers house.[1] He took his journey into a far country, leaving behind the authority figure in his life. I personally believe he was trying to get as far away from the authority in his life as he could.

The Word of God says he began to spend his inheritance on riotous living, pleasing and gratifying the flesh. The more the flesh was gratified, the farther away from the father's house he went, away from the authority in his life. Soon he was totally separated from his Father and his sensuality began to appease him. The word says in James 1:15, "then after desire has conceived, it gives birth to sin and sin when it is full grown gives birth to death."[2] Is it wrong to desire things? No, but we need to be wise and count the cost of the full measure if it goes unchecked; or have a moral compass of the consequences!

Frank Sinatra sang the song *My Way* made popular in 1969. The English lyrics were written by Paul Anka. The last verse says

> *Regrets? I've had a few,*
> *but then again, too few to mention,*
> *I did what I had to do and saw it though*
> *without exemption*
> *I planned each chartered course, each careful step*
> *along the byway - but more, much more than this:*
> *I did it my way!*

I found out the hard way, doing it my way was not the plan of God for my life. Regrets were more - much more - than a few for me, and they were too many to list. What I do recall was that when I came to the end of my rope, satan was there - being very persuasive, trying to take my life.

Thank God there was an exemption for me as Holy Spirit was there as well, offering me an exchange of life! He said: 'you give me your life in exchange for what I will give you' as He ministered to me.[3]

The temptations in your life are no different from what others experience. God is faithful. He will not allow the temptation to be more than you can stand. When you are tempted, He will show you a way out so that you can endure. I repented of my sins, rededicated my life to Jesus with a determination to follow Him the rest of my life.

The book of James begins by telling us to count it all joy when we fall into divers' temptations. Knowing that the testing of our faith produces patience, but let patience have its perfect work that you may be perfect and complete lacking nothing.[4] When we go through the "proper" process we become fully developed, lacking nothing! They that wait upon the Lord shall renew their strength they shall mount up with wings like eagles they shall run and not be weary they shall walk and not faint or become tired.[5]

When we wait upon the Lord (look for, expect, and hope in Him) We will draw close to Him like eagles mounting up to the sun, and He supplies our needs according to His riches in glory.[6] My pastor, Reverend Brian Matthews says, "God may not always bless the plans you have, so why not choose the plan that God has for you, as it is already blessed."

---

1. Luke 15:13 KJV
2. James 1:15 NIV
3. 1 Corinthians 10:13 NLT
4. James 1:2-4 KJV
5. Isaiah 40:31 KJV
6. Philippians 4:19 KJV

CHAPTER 3
SEPARATION

When we are pulled away by self will, we are moved from patience to selfishness. We fail and become vulnerable. We lose our sober mind set and are not on alert as we should be. We become prey for the enemy to devour. 1 Peter 5:8 tells us be well balanced (temperate, sober of mind), be vigilant and cautious at all times; for that enemy of yours, the devil, roams around like a roaring lion (in fierce hunger), seeking someone to seize upon and devour.[1] Our tests and trials come to make us strong, but we must allow patience to have its perfect work, if we are to be perfect, complete, and lacking nothing.[2] The Lord God is a sun and shield, the Lord will give grace and glory, no good thing will He withhold from them that walk uprightly.[3] The Father knows how to give good gifts! We must learn how to receive and care for the gifts He gives, for we are His workmanship, created in Christ Jesus for good works.[4]

Like many who drift away from the Father, the prodigal son story closely parallels the downward spiral that life, distant from the Father, will lead us. Just as the prodigal came to destruction in his quest for freedom, and the opportunity to "do it his way," spiritual destruction will come to all who find themselves separated from God.

If you have ever tasted the goodness of God, you are never satisfied until you return to Him. O taste and see that the Lord is good.[5] Famine is sure to come to anyone who has been in the Father's house yet has left the Father's house.

The Holy Spirit will pull at your heart ever so gently and bring conviction of sin in your life. Holy Spirit will call you back to oneness with the Father, back into relationship with Him.

God misses the time you once gave Him and the time you spent with Him. He loves you more than you could ever imagine. If you find yourself in this position or place in life, I can almost hear you saying *"yes, I know God loves me but..."* It isn't 'He loves you but...' It's actually: He loves you and He wants you to return home!

He is waiting for you, my brother, my sister - God knows where you are. That's why the Holy Spirit has convicted your heart! You belong to God; you are His child; He loves you no matter what you have done. God does not condemn us, that is not his nature. Satan condemns and accuses us. Satan lies to us and wants us to believe that God doesn't love or care for us, but God is Love, He loves you. Because He loves you, *because He loves you*: that's what He is, He doesn't change, God is Love.

You may have faults, but you're in good company. Moses committed murder. He disobeyed God by striking the rock when God commanded him to speak to the rock, yet God loved him.[6]

What about David? He committed adultery, then committed murder,[7] yet God loved him and said of him he is a man after My own heart![8]

How about Peter: he was the reed (Simon) that became the rock (Peter). When Jesus asked "Who do you say that I am?" Simon Peter replied, "You are the Christ, the Son of the living God." Then Jesus answered him, "Blessed are you, Simon, son of Jonah, because flesh and blood did not reveal this to you, but my Father who is in heaven. I say unto you that you are Peter and upon this rock, (foundational truth, this revelation) I will build my church and the gates of hades will not overpower it![9] Yet, Peter cursed and denied Christ.[10] Jesus declared to him, "Peter, I have prayed for you that your faith fail not and when you return to me, strengthen your brethren.[11]

Then there's Saul, the Christian murderer,[12] whom God chose to be an apostle, and changed his name to Paul.[13] He wrote two-thirds of the New Testament!

Friend, God can and will take our mess and make it a message, but we must realize we are accepted in the Beloved. God never condemns us for falling. Jesus was the only one that was without sin. When the religious leaders brought a woman to Him that was caught in adultery,[14] they set her in the midst of them and said to Jesus, "This woman was caught in the very act. Now Moses in the law commanded us that such should be stoned, but what do you say?"

They were trying to trap Jesus and find fault in Him concerning the law. They were searching for something to accuse Him of. Jesus stooped down and wrote on the ground with His finger as though He did not hear them. When they continued asking Him, He raised himself up and said to them, "He who is without sin among you, let him throw the first stone." Again He stooped down and wrote on the ground. Then those who heard it, being convicted by their conscience, went out one by one, beginning with the oldest even to the last.

Jesus was left alone with the woman standing in the midst. When Jesus raised himself up and saw no one but the woman, He asked "Woman where are those accusers of yours? Has no one condemned you"?

She said, "No one, Lord"

Jesus said to her, "Neither do I condemn you. Go and sin no more."

He was the only one that could have literally stoned the woman, but He gave her mercy instead of condemnation.

Satan is the accuser of the brethren. He will always try to make us feel unworthy, unfit, and tell us God doesn't love us or want anything to do with us. Satan is a liar and the father of lies. The devil realizes if we wear the name of Christ and look into the word of God long enough, we will become what we behold. An example is: if you drink too much alcohol you are labeled as an alcoholic; if you commit adultery, you are labeled as an adulterer. If you steal, you are labeled as a thief and so on. You may have done all these things, But God!!! He said old things have passed away and behold all things have become new.[15]

Begin to look at yourself in a new way, a new light! Begin to see yourself as God sees you: the finished product that He has called you to be. Now move toward what you behold! God wants to do a new thing in your life, He is calling out to you to return to Him, He knows where you are this very moment and what has caused you to separate yourself from Him, yet He continues to pursue you because you belong to Him.

A free gift has been presented to you! Accept it! Open it up, and you will experience a whole new world. There is a place reserved for you,. It has your name on it. No one can occupy it but you. No one can do your part in the Kingdom - won't you accept the invitation to return?

Why is it that we so often continue in misery? Self-abasement settles in, so we try this, and that, or the other, to feel better. Many times fall ing right back into the trap that God has already delivered us from, only to find ourselves starving for God. It's time to realize who you are called to be according to 1 Peter 2:9 "But you are a chosen generation, a royal priest-hood a Holy nation. Gods on special people, that you may proclaim the praises of Him who called you out of darkness into His marvelous light."[16]

You see, you were called to come out of darkness into the light because you are God's workmanship. He wants to use your testimony to bring to those wandering in the wilderness of darkness into the marvelous light of Jesus Christ.

When you become starved for more of God, just a word will bring you to your senses. In that moment, you realize: 'in my Fathers' house there is more than enough.'

It is here we become humbled by our circumstances. It is here we realize slopping the hogs in the pig pen is no place for a blood bought child of the living God.

It is time to get up, come to your senses and return to where your provision comes from. The same road that led you to the pig pen, in the opposite direction, will lead you back to the Fathers house.

---

1. 1 Peter 5:8 AMP
2. James 1:4 KJV
3. Psalms 84:11 KJV
4. Eph. 2:10 KJV
5. Psalms 34:8 KJV
6. Num.20: 8-12 KVJ

7. 2 Sam.11:5-16 KJV
8. 1 Sam.13:14 KJV
9. Matt. 16: 13 AMP
10. Mark 14:71 AMP
11. Luke 22:32 KJV
12. Acts 9:1 KJV
13. Acts 13:9 KJV
14. John 8:4-11 KJV
15. 2 Corinthians 5:17 KVJ
16. 1 Peter 2:9 KJV

CHAPTER 4
SPIRITUAL DESTRUCTION

The prodigal son was having a good time living it up, not caring or preparing for the future. The Bible says he wasted his fortune in reckless and loose (free from restraint) living. He had, you might say, bought friendship. As long as he had money and was sharing it with everyone around with whomever he desired, he had friends. He was enjoying his inheritance with no consideration for the future. His happiness and strength were in his possessions. When his possessions ran out, there went the happiness and strength with them. He was living among Gentiles, so no one was reminding him of his past or asking about his Father.

Living life in this way was bound to end abruptly. Resources run out when there is constant withdrawals and no deposits made. Our joy does not come from our possessions. The Joy of the Lord is our strength.[1]

When we feel sorrow, whether it is due to the realization of sin or because of difficult circumstances, we may wonder where our strength is going to come from. It is vital to remember the joy of the Lord is our strength. This type of joy does not come from our circumstances, our possessions, or something we conjure up within ourselves. It comes from one source only - the Lord.

It's so amazing that God-given joy centers around us. Hebrews 12:2 says that Jesus endured the cross, "for the joy set before Him"(meaning he endured the cross to have a relationship with us).

Zephaniah 3:17 says that God rejoices over us with singing! Think about this fact: being in relationship with you makes God happy! Knowing that God feels this way about you should spark the flame of joy within you!

As Christians we have access to God's boundless joy, a joy that does not come from our circumstances or within ourselves. It does not depend on how strong or how spiritual we are. This joy comes from God alone, and the relationship we have with Him. If we find ourselves disconnected from God, then joy and strength are gone.

The loss of joy and strength is often followed by self-abasement. This means being humbled by consciousness of inferiority; to feel unworthiness; guilt; or shame. Oftentimes at this place the experience of hope is gone. The heart is full of sorrow, and the individual cannot believe how much they have let God down.

This is the point where the enemy begins to pile on the condemnation and build a case against the individual in their own mind, attempting to make you think God no longer cares about you. Thoughts arise, saying that you have gone too far for God to reach you; that you should just give up and not even try to return to God because He doesn't love you anymore. Let me remind you what Jesus said about Satan: he is a liar and the father of lies and all that is false.

Understand that God called you with a heavenly calling. He knows the end from the beginning,[2]therefore the events in your life along the way have not taken God by surprise. They may have taken you by surprise, but not God, He knows all! "I knew you before I formed you in your mothers' womb. Before you were born, I set you apart and appointed you."[3] Your fall did not surprise God the Father.

When we find ourselves destitute of the things of God, it makes us feel unworthy - and we are unworthy on our own - but Jesus shed his blood that we could become worthy! He paid the penalty for our sin. Guilt is used by the enemy to bring shame upon us for falling, but when you return to the Fathers' house you can leave that shame at the door. It isn't welcome in the Fathers' house! If we confess our sin, He is faithful and just to forgive us our sins and to cleanse us from all unrighteousness.[4] For I will forgive their wickedness and will remember their sins no more.[5] As far as the east is from the west so far has he removed our transgressions from us.[6]

Do not lie down at the feet of spiritual destruction and give up! When we mess-up we need to get up and run as fast as we can into the Fathers arms and repent! It's not a license to sin, but it is because we are human, and we fail God!

There is hope, joy unspeakable and full of glory waiting for you. There is no doubt in my mind that the Holy Spirit has been pursuing you and gently nudging you to come to the Father, that is what He does. He wants to see you restored, whole and complete, wanting nothing. It is your move; God has beckoned you to come home.

In 2 Kings 7:3 there were four men with leprosy at the entrance of the city gate.[7] They said to each other, "Why stay here until we die? If we say, 'we will enter the city,' then the famine is in the city and we shall die there, and if we sit still here, we die also. So now come, let us go over to the army of the Syrians. If they spare us alive, we shall live and if they kill us, we shall but die. So, they arose in the twilight and went to the Syrian camp. but when they came to the edge of the camp, no man was there. For the Lord had made the Syrian army hear a noise of chariots and horses, the noise of a great army. They have said to one another 'the King of Israel has hired the Hittite and Egyptian kings to come upon us.' So, the Syrians arose and fled in the twilight and left their tents, horses, donkeys, even the camp as it was, they fled for their lives.

When God is fighting for you, there is no reason to draw back from entering in. He tells us to come boldly to the throne of grace. Let us then fearlessly and confidently and boldly draw near to the throne of grace that we may receive mercy and find grace to help in good time for every need.[8]

Jesus paid it all on calvary. Restoration is a gift waiting for you! Open it and enjoy the benefits. God has not called you to sit on the side lines and watch others do the work. He placed a call upon your life because you have what it takes to reach others for the kingdom of Christ.

Now is the time to get up and get moving in what God has called you to do. It is not enough to be hearers only. God wants us to be doers of the word.[9] But someone will say, 'you have faith; I have deeds.'

Show me your faith without deeds, and I will show you my faith by my deeds.

---

1. Neh. 8:10 KJV
2. Isaiah 46:10 KJV
3. Jeremiah 1:5 KJV
4. 1 John 1:9 NIV

5. Hebrews 8:12 NIV
6. Psalms 193:12 NIV
7. 2 Kings 7:3 NIV
8. Heb. 4:16 AMP
9. James 2:18 NIV

CHAPTER 5
RECONCILIATION

The prodigal son reached the lowest place a Jewish individual could find themselves: in the pig pen feeding swine. He had reached a place of destitution. He had no money, no friends, no family. No man gave him anything.[1] Therefore he was starving. When no man gives you anything and you find that the slop of this world can not satisfy, you will come to your senses. You will realize there is still provision in the Father's house and even the servants are provided for.

You may feel as this prodigal felt: *"I will return to my father's house and ask him to make me a servant because I am no longer worthy to be called a son."* Yet I tell you the truth: just as the prodigal sons' father was anticipating his return, looking for him consistently, God is also doing for *you*. He is waiting, watching, and anticipating your return. When you do decide to return to the Father's house, He will welcome you with open arms, put a robe on you, put a ring on your finger and shoes on your feet.

When the prodigal son left the pig pen that day, the stench of the pigs upon him, he began the journey to return to the Fathers house. I believe he knew his father would be forgiving.

He probably felt that dad would make him like a hired servant in his home. I'm sure along the way he rehearsed over and over in his mind what he would say to his father. *"I have sinned against heaven and you, but can you forgive me and make me a servant, I am hungry and destitute and in need."*

There was a Jewish law that stated: if a son lost his inheritance among Gentiles and then returned home, the community would perform a ceremony, called the kezazah. They would have a large gathering, break a large pot in front of him and yell. *"You are cut off from your people!"* The community would totally reject him.

The prodigal son was willing to take his chance of being humiliated by the community in order to be reconciled to his father, whether as a son or a servant.

As he made his journey homeward, his father saw him 'a long way off' which meant he was looking for him. Seeing him 'afar off,' the father ran to him. This tells me the father never stopped looking for his son to return. The father shamed himself by running to meet his son. It was considered a shame for a man to lift his tunic and run, but the father had taken on the full shame that should have fallen to his son. This clearly showed the entire community that his son was welcome back home.

In the parable, only the father could restore his son to full sonship. Once the father restored his son, the community could not hold a kezazah ceremony. There would be no rejecting this son --- despite what he had done! The Father did not ask his son, *"Where have you been? What have you done with your inheritance?"* or, *"Why are you coming back here now?"* No, the Father wanted to cover his sons' sin and shame by not exposing him. It did not matter to the Father that the son had nothing to show for his share of the inheritance. What mattered was his that son had returned home.

I like what Prophet Ed Traut said about the father, *"He didn't tell his servants, go run the bath water so we can scrub him down and make a bon fire to burn his clothes because he stinks. He sent them for the best robe to be put on him, a ring on his finger and shoes on his feet, to show the servants of the house this my son has returned, and he has been restored to his position as a son in the house."* Then he went even further: 'bring the fattened calf and kill it! Let's have a feast and celebrate. For this son of mine was dead and is alive, has was lost and is found.'

The father never acknowledged what the son said, *"I have sinned against heaven and against you and I am no longer worthy to be called your son."* To the father, the very fact that his son had returned showed he had a repentant heart. Instead, he adorned him in a robe of royalty, and put a ring on his finger which was a symbol of authority, unity, sonship and love. He put shoes on his feet to identify him as royalty and not a slave.

So often we, from a fallen standpoint, will come to the Father and say, *"Lord I am no longer worthy to be called your son, if I can just make it into heaven, that's my only desire."* Brother, Sister, Friend: when God restores you, your work must be completed, your call is without repentance. If man appoints you to a position, then man can demote you, but when God calls you and places His anointing upon you, He will place you where He wants you. If you will be pliable in His hands, He can get the glory from your gifting and calling.

Heaven rejoices over one sinner coming into the Kingdom, so heaven rejoices when a prodigal returns home. In the story of the prodigal son the father threw a party and killed the fattened calf because his son had returned home. The very fact that he returned said he was sorry for what he had done! In Luke 15:25-32, we read about the older brother who was in the field. When he came near the house, he heard music and dancing (rejoicing). He asked one of the servants what was going on. *"Your brother has come home,"* he replied, *"and your father has killed the fattened calf because he has him back safe and sound."* The older brother became angry and refused to go in. So, his father went out and pleaded with him, but he answered his father, *"Look all these years I've been slaving for you and never once disobeyed your orders. Yet you never gave me even a young goat so I could celebrate with my friends. But when this son of yours who has squandered your property with prostitutes comes home, you kill the fattened calf for him!"[2]*

"My son," the father said, *"you are always with me, and everything I have is yours. But we had to celebrate and be glad, because this brother of yours was dead and is alive again, he was lost and is found!"*

Yet the older brother refused to go in and take part in the celebration. The older brother did not care for his father, and didn't care to take part in his father's joy. His heart was not with the father.

He had the work ethic down, but he did not have a relationship with his father. If he had, he would have rejoiced in the fact that the father was happy concerning the return of his younger brother.

The Older Brother Syndrome is often played out in the lives of professing Christians. Those with this condition feel as though they have never sinned as bad as the prodigal. They might attend a the church where a prodigal has returned, however, they will stand in the way of the prodigal from moving in the gift and call of God on that person's life. They boldly proclaim, *"Oh, he can't teach because of his past sin. He can't be ordained in this movement because of his past. He can't do this, or that ..."*

Wait a minute! God's Word declares that when God forgives us, He put our sins as far away from us as the east is from the west, so far has He removed our transgressions from us.[3] God said, "for they shall know Me, from the least of them unto the greatest of them, saith the Lord: for I will forgive their iniquity, and I will remember their sin no more."[4]

Friend, when God forgives, He does not bring the sin back up! It is forgiven and forgotten. There is no record of that sin.

I once asked God *"why do Your people love to bring up brothers' and sisters' past failures?"* God said to me, *"I am not the accuser of the brethren my son, once I forgive, I cannot bring it back up because I do not remember it anymore. If someone reminds you of a past sin it is not me! No matter what label the individual is wearing. Satan is the accuser of the brethren and oftentimes people do his business of accusing!"*

I got so excited, I did a little dance right where I was! Isn't it exciting to know that God does not keep a record of our forgiven sin? Man will always remember your failures, but God doesn't! His blood cleanses us from all unrighteousness and we become brand new.

Come now, and let us reason together, saith the Lord: though your sins be as scarlet, they shall be white as snow, though they be red like crimson, they shall be as wool. Isaiah 1:18

---

1. Luke 15:16 KJV
2. Luke 15:25-32 NIV
3. Psalms 103:12 NIV
4. Jeremiah 31:34 NIV

CHAPTER 6
THE ROBE

Forgiveness would be empty without restoration to the privileges forfeited by sin from the very beginning. Therefore, if you bear the name 'son' or 'daughter' through having received Jesus as Lord and Savior by the power of the Holy Spirit, you have found favor with the Father.

The best robe has been placed on you as a demonstration of the Fathers' complete approval, His love and protection for you. You are an heir of God and a joint heir with Christ Jesus who has been appointed heir of all things[1]

God places on us the robe of righteousness when we come to Him and *then* He cleans us up. The grave clothes are traded out for garments of salvation. I will greatly rejoice in the Lord, my soul shall be joyful in my God; for He hath clothed me with the garments of salvation, He hath covered me with the robe of righteousness as a bridegroom decks himself with ornaments, and as a bride adorns herself with her jewels.[2]

We may come back to God broken, with our life in shambles; disheartened by our faults and failures; regretting our mistake. God takes all of that and trades it for a life fitly put back together. With Him at the center, we go from the altar being altered with a robe of righteousness. Restored: not as in 'rebuffed and re-polished' but as the old being made new.

Therefore, if any man be in Christ, he is a new creature, old things are passed away; behold, all things have become new.[3] Christ will change the way you talk, the way you walk, the way you act, and He will change your very countenance. The robe of righteousness declares you the righteousness of God.

He made Christ who knew no sin to be sin on our behalf, so that in Him we would become the righteousness of God.[4]

The Spirit of the Lord God is upon me: because he hath anointed me to preach good tidings unto the meek: he hath sent me to bind up the brokenhearted, to proclaim liberty to the captives, and the opening of the prison to them that are bound; To proclaim the acceptable year of the Lord, and the day of vengeance of our God; to comfort all that mourn; to appoint unto them that mourn in Zion, to give them beauty for ashes, the oil of joy for mourning, the garment of praise for the Spirit of heaviness; that they may be called trees of righteousness, the planting of the Lord, that he might be glorified.[5]

Friend, if you are still waiting to decide to return to the Father's house, do it now! Just ask God with a sincere heart to forgive you, to cleanse you from all unrighteousness. If you will confess with your mouth the Lord Jesus and shall believe in your heart that God has raised Him from the dead, you shall be saved! For with the heart man believes unto righteousness; and with the mouth confession is made unto salvation. For the scripture says, Whosoever, shall call upon the name of the Lord shall be saved.[6]

With that robe of righteousness comes authority. Jesus said, behold, I give unto you power (Greek word *exousia* meaning authority) to tread on serpents and scorpions, and over all the power (Greek word for this one is *dynamis* meaning strength power, ability) of the enemy and nothing shall by any means hurt you. [7]

Jesus has given us authority over the powers of darkness. Authority in His name to: cast out devils, to cleanse the lepers and raise the dead.

The enemy will put us to the test to see if we know we have that authority, and to see if we will use our authority to stop his advances.

When we do not use our God given authority, we are like an armed police officer in a bank. When a robber comes in to rob the bank and the officer just stands there and says, *"I know they see me standing here in my uniform, with a gun on my side, what do they think they are doing?"* while the bank robber is steadily holding up the tellers and stealing the money. When the officer does not enforce the authority he has been given, that bank gets robbed and the robbers get away with the goods.

We must take our position of authority in Christ and petition God on how to use the weapons of our warfare, for they are not carnal, but they are mighty through God to the pulling down of strong holds. [8]

When the enemy looks at us, as we are in Christ, he knows we have been given the *exousia* (authority) of Jesus Christ in our life. He hopes that we don't know it, or know how to use it! He does not care if we look like the church, as long as we don't do the works that Christ did. He does not want us to be doers of the Word of God.

It is time for the Church to rise-up and use this God given authority and take back what the enemy has stolen from us. We have dropped our guard. The enemy has played havoc in the lives of many believers, who do not know their authority in Christ.

We must pray and seek God on how to use the arsenal God has given us against the wiles of the devil. We war not against flesh and blood but against principalities, against powers, against the rulers of darkness of this world, against spiritual wickedness in high places.[9]

As a result of not recognizing the enemy's tactics, we rival against one another with racial issues, hypocrisy, slander, and false accusations. When we know the Word of God, we realize the enemy wants us at war against one another, turning on one another, to destroy one another.

Let us turn our focus to the spirit behind what is luring us to come against our brothers and sisters and realize there is a devil loose that God has given us authority over - and come against that spirit. We destroy one another when we should be destroying the powers of darkness with the weapons of our warfare.

It's time to shake off the grave clothes and robe up with the righteousness of God.

---

1. Romans 8:17 NIV, Hebrews 1:2 NIV
2. Isaiah 61:10 KJV
3. 2 Corinthians 5:17 KJV
4. 2 Corinthians 5:21 AM
5. Isaiah 61:1-3 KJV
6. Romans 10:9-11 KJV
7. Luke 10:19 KJV
8. 2 Corinthians 10:4 KJV
9. Ephesians 6:12 KJV

CHAPTER 7

THE RING OF
RECONCILIATION

The father of the prodigal son called for a ring to be placed upon his son's finger. The ring was recognition that the son was accepted, greatly loved, and forgiven.

Through the Bible rings were given as a sign of authority. We see often in the Old Testament that kings had a signet ring as a sign of authority. In Gen. 41:37-42 Pharaoh gave Joseph his signet ring as a sign of the authority he had given him, after Joseph interpreted Pharaoh's dream. Joseph was promoted to second in command in Pharaoh's kingdom. He wore the king's signet ring, and the finest robes were placed upon him. This happened because he relied upon the wisdom of God and was obedient to his call despite all the obstacles he had to go through to get to where he was.

When you return and find favor with God, symbolically a ring of reconciliation is placed upon you, representing the riches you have in Christ. It also represents the authority you have been given in the name of Jesus. God has called us to be kings and priest for him, so we step into the office of King and Priest to God.

As we come to the realization that we have authority in Christ and study the Word to learn how to operate in this God given authority, we will then begin to walk in victory.

God has not given us a spirit of fear, but of power of love and a sound mind.[1] Fear comes in many forms and fashions. We could say the prodigal son feared his father would not recognize him as a son because of his sin or his riotous living, therefore he would ask to be made a servant.

Fear separates us one from another. Fear divides homes, marriages, businesses, and relationships. Fear brings destruction of lives and often leaves behind its' evidence. Fear is an accuser. The insecurities of one individual, may cause another to be accused of something that is not a reality.

Fear creates distrust because it is false evidence appearing real. There is no fear in love, but perfect love cast out fear, for fear has torment, and he that fears has not been made perfect in love.[2] We have received the perfect love of God, and His perfect love casts out fear.

We have been given power - which is strength and ability not of our own, but of God; a power consisting in, or resting upon armies, forces, and host. This is depicted in 2 Kings 6:15-17: "When the servant of the man of God was risen early, and gone forth, behold, an host compassed the city both with horses and chariots. And his servant said unto him, *'Alas, my master! How shall we do?'* And he answered, *'Fear not for they that be with us are more than they that be with them.'* And Elisha prayed and said Lord, I pray thee, open his eyes, that he may see. And the Lord opened the eyes of the young man; and he saw: and behold the mountain was full of horses and chariots of fire round about Elisha.

We have been given love, the agape love of God: a love that is not based upon merit or favor, it is unconditional love. God loves you because that is what He is. God is Love. He can't *not* love you because He is Love. Even if you don't love Him, He still loves you. We have been given a sound mind, which is self-control or the capacity of moderation. We can no longer use the excuse "that is just who I am" to act out, or be out of control.

We receive the jewels in the ring of reconciliation and allow these jewels to begin to manifest in our lives. They produce through us the hope of glory for all those we meet.

In the book of Romans chapter five, Paul speaks of eight things that we have received when we are justified through faith. In the remaining chapters, we will look at these jewels, listed in the *Thompson Chain Reference Bible* as the *Eight Jewels in the Ring of Reconciliation*.

---

1. 2 Timothy 1:7 KJV
2. 1 John 4:18 KJV

CHAPTER 8
JEWEL OF PEACE

Romans 5:12 states: *"Therefore being justified by faith, we have peace with God through our Lord Jesus Christ."* Being justified - meaning, just as if I had never sinned - provides restoration and right standing with God.

It is by faith we believe and hold the conviction that God exists and is the Creator and Ruler of all things. He is the Provider, and bestows eternal salvation through Christ. Through faith we have peace with God. The word *have* comes from the Greek word *echo* [pronounced e'kho]. It is a verb, meaning:

1. To have (hold in the hand, in the sense of wearing)
2. To have (hold) possession of the mind (refers to alarm, agitating emotions, etc.)
3. To wear or possess the peace of God.

Peace comes from the Greek word *eirene*, [pronounced a-ra'-na] and is a feminine noun meaning:

1. *A state of national tranquility*
2. *Exemption from rage and havoc of war.*

3. *Peace between individuals, i.e. harmony, concord.*
4. *Of Christianity, the tranquil state of a soul assured of its salvation through Christ, and so fearing nothing from God and content with its earthly lot of whatsoever sort that is.*

Basically, the type of peace and contentment that passes all understanding between God and His child, even when there is chaos all around, describes this jewel of peace. It is ours. Jesus said, *"Peace I leave with you, my peace I give unto you: not as the world giveth, give I unto you. Let not your heart be troubled, neither let it be afraid."*[1]

"Do not let your faith waver, neither allow fear to grasp your heart, because that is grounds for enemy to play havoc with your emotions," is essentially what Jesus was telling us. Being justified comes through faith not feelings. With the peace of God in our life we will be exempt from raging emotions of uneasiness, worry and strife.

Returning to the Father brings comfort in knowing that the Father is pleased with you. The world cannot offer peace without compromise, but Jesus gives us peace unconditionally because He loves us.

The peace of God cannot be bought - it is freely given to us from Jesus. *He was wounded for our transgressions, bruised for our iniquities and the chastisement of our peace was upon him.*[2] Therefore, when we accept Christ as our Lord and Savior, we receive *the peace of God that passes all understanding.*[3] This peace allows us to stand after we have done all to stand, *having our loins gird about with truth and having on the breast plate of righteousness*[4] while we wait upon the manifestation of what is being sought after.

The enemy tries to rob us of our peace by causing a scene, stirring up strife, and even twisting our words to be interpreted entirely different than what has been said! Satan does not want you to have peace, he wants you to fear life itself. If he can get you to operate in fear, he can create havoc in your life because fear has torment.

When we fear what is not seen, we begin to speak about it as if we know how bad it is, or how bad it will be. Often, we speak our fears into existence. The Bible says we shall have what we say, therefore if we are in fear, we speak things into being that should not be. This causes worry and anxiety in our life, and therefore causes us to doubt God.

Therefore, the Jewel of Peace is given to us in love, and the perfect love of God cast out all fear.[5]

---

1. John 14:27 KJV
2. Isaiah 53:5 KJV
3. Philippians 4:7 KJV
4. Ephesians 6:14 KJV
5. 1 John 4:18 KJV

CHAPTER 9
JEWEL OF ACCESS

Romans 5:2 states: "By whom also we have access by faith into this grace wherein we stand and rejoice in hope of the glory of God."

This jewel brings us into the very presence of God, where we can be seated in heavenly places in Christ Jesus.[1] We serve an approachable God who extends to us grace. This grace is something we cannot buy. It is something we cannot earn. No matter how good you have been, you can never earn grace! Grace was bought and paid for by Jesus, therefore we must access it by faith.

Grace provides us with what we do not deserve: the forgiveness of our sins and eternal life.

And now, because we are united in Christ, we both have equal and direct access in the realm of the Holy Spirit to come before the Father.[2] We have boldness through Him. We also have free access as kings and priests before the Father because of our complete confidence in Christ's faithfulness.[3] We can approach God and make our petitions known to him through the Holy Spirit. He hears and answers prayer.

This access allows us to have dialog with God. We talk to Him, and He talks back to us. So now we come freely and boldly to where love is enthroned, to receive mercy's kiss and discover the grace we urgently need to strengthen us in our time of weakness.[4]

We can come boldly to the throne of grace, and receive mercy. Mercy keeps us from getting what we deserve! It is the mercy of God that cancels the sentence of eternity in hell off our life. Before God's throne is where that we discover the grace that we need to make it through difficult places, and when we feel guilt, rejection, disappointment, and heartache.

The grace of God that bestows the love of the Father upon us changes our life. Graham Cooke said:

> The Father loves you, because He loves you, because He loves you! Because that is what He is! He is love, and He can't see you any other way. If you decide to never return to Him and walk straight into hell, He loves you. God is love and He longs to lavish His love on you. He will not force himself on you, you were born with your own free will, and you must make that decision to choose life.

God said in Deuteronomy 30:19, "I call heaven and earth to record this day against you, that I have set before Life and death, blessing and cursing: therefore choose life, that both you and your seed may live."

We have access to the Holy of Holies! Come, let us rejoice in the Lord and give thanks to His Holy name for providing us access.

---

1. Ephesians 2:6 KJV

2. Ephesians 2:18 TPT
3. Ephesians 3:12 TPT
4. Hebrews 4:16 TPT

CHAPTER 10
THE JEWEL OF JOY IN HOPE

We have joy in the knowledge that God is for us. If God be for you, who can stand against you and prosper? We have a hope in Christ that goes beyond normal wishful thinking.

God gives us joy unspeakable and full of glory. "To provide for those who grieve in Zion, to bestow on them a crown of beauty instead of ashes, the oil of joy instead of morning, and a garment of praise instead of a spirit of despair, they will be called oaks of righteousness, a planting of the Lord for the display of his splendor."[1]

Restoration brings freedom, freedom produces joy in the Lord, who has made us free. Nehemiah instructed the people: "This day is holy to our Lord. Do not grieve, for the joy of the Lord is your strength."[2] He was encouraging the people and reminding them that they had hope. God would see them through the task that lie ahead of them.

We, too, must understand that we have joy in hope. Our joy does not come from the circumstances that surround us, our joy comes from being secure in the Father's love, and this security produces hope that tomorrow will be better than today. For *"without hope we are of all men most miserable."*[3]

When the prodigal son came to himself, he had a revelation of what he had at his father's house. He remembered that even the servants had it better than he had it at that moment. The servants' needs where supplied. They did not want or lack for anything! So, he got up and went to his father's house, because of the hope that sprung up in him through his renewed revelation. Joy was the product of his hope once the connection with the father was made.

When you are called of God and a disconnect takes place because of sin, life becomes miserable. The lies of the enemy seem to get louder and louder. The enemy attempts to convince you there is no need to pursue God any longer with his lies, saying: *"Look what you have done! You will never preach again! You'll never teach again! You'll never sing under the anointing again!"* The lies apply to whatever it is you are called to do. The devil is a liar, and the father of lies.[4]

God is still in the business of restoration, so stop procrastinating! Hope deferred (meaning delayed, stretched out, or put off), makes the heart sick: but when the desire cometh, (when restoration, forgiveness, and repentance comes), it is a tree of life.[5] Don't put it off another minute my brother; my sister! Rise up respond to the pull of the Holy Spirit! Come to the Father!

Let us therefore come boldly to the throne of grace, that we may obtain mercy and find grace to help in the time of need.[6] Let go of your faults, lay aside your failures, and ask God to forgive you. He is faithful and just to forgive.

Allow God to restore unto you the joy of your salvation - He is looking for you. The Holy Spirit is dealing with your heart even now, to come home. There is no condemnation to a repentant heart. God extends the oil of joy,[7] so bring your brokenness in hope and you will find joy in restoration. The Father is waiting!

God's love is unconditional, so it doesn't matter what you have done, how far you have gone, or what the issues are that you face. Simply come as you are. Let the water of God's Word wash over you[8] He will cleanse you from all unrighteousness and make you whole and complete in Him. David said in Psalms: "Restore unto me the joy of your salvation and sustain me with a willing spirit."[9] Be the one with a spirit that is seeking after God, and then your mouth will declare His praise. You will be a testimony of what the Lord has done.

Allow God to take your failures and mistakes and craft them into a message that will teach others about the goodness of our God. God deserves our praise! He is worthy to be praised. When He brings us out of darkness into His marvelous light[10] we become a royal diadem for Him: a royal priesthood, a chosen generation, a holy nation, a peculiar people that should show forth praises of our God.[11]

We are a people that have obtained mercy, therefore we should give Him praise. Jesus said in Luke, concerning the woman that washed His feet with her tears and wiped them with her hair: *"Wherefore I say unto thee, her sins, which are many, are forgiven: for she loved much: but unto whom little is forgiven, the same loveth little.*[12]

Basically, where there is much forgiven there is much love. I can't speak for anyone else, but He reached way below the bottom when He reached down and set me free. There was much forgiven. Now there is much love, as well as much thanksgiving.

He said if we don't praise Him the rocks would cry out[13] and I simply won't allow a rock to cry out in my place! I'm going to praise Him for what He has done for me! He gives joy unspeakable and full of glory.[14]

God is ready to bring full restoration to your life, won't you surrender your all to Him? Will you allow Him to come in and make your heart His home?

---

1. Isaiah 61:3 TPT
2. Nehemiah 8:10 TPT
3. 1 Corinthians 5:19 KJV
4. John 8:44 KJV
5. Proverbs 13:12 KJV
6. Hebrews 4:16 KJV
7. Isaiah 61:3 KJV
8. Ephesians 5:26 KJV
9. Psalms 51:12 AMP
10. 1 Peter 2:9 KJV
11. 1 Peter 2:9 KJV
12. Luke 7:47 KJV
13. Luke 19:40 KJV
14. 1 Peter 1:8 KJV

CHAPTER 11

THE JEWEL OF JOY IN SUFFERING

God wants to give you the Fruit of the Spirit, which is love, joy, peace, long-suffering, gentleness, goodness, faith, meekness, and temperance. Against such there is no law.[1] This fruit is produced in the life of a believer. It is processed as we go through life. We learn that, whatever we must go through, God is right there with us and he will see us through with joy (an assurance) even in the suffering.

When Paul and Silas were beaten and thrown in jail, held in stocks for preaching the gospel, they didn't give up and decide "maybe it will be best if we don't speak in the name of Jesus any more…" No, rather, they prayed and sang praises unto God. Their fellow prisoners heard them. Suddenly there was a great earthquake, so strong that the foundations of the prison were shaken. Immediately all the doors were opened, and every one's bands were loosed. The keeper of the prison, awaking out of his sleep, seeing the prison doors open, drew out his sword, and would have killed himself, supposing that the prisoners had fled. But Paul cried with a loud voice saying, 'Do thyself no harm: for we are all here!' Then the guard called for a light, and sprang in, trembling, and fell down before Paul and Silas. As they were brought them out, and said 'Sirs, what must I do to be saved?' And they said, 'Believe on the Lord Jesus Christ, and thou shall be saved, and they house.'" Then they spoke unto him the word of the Lord, and to all that were in his house. He took them the same hour of the night and washed their stripes, and was baptized, he and all his, straightway.[2]

The life of this jailer and all his family was changed because two men of God counted their trial as joy in suffering for Christ's sake. Through the sufferings of Christ our salvation was made perfect. But we see Jesus, who was made a little lower than the angels for the suffering of death, crowned with glory and honor: that He, by the grace of God, should taste death for every man. For it became Him, for whom are all things, and by whom are all things, in bringing many sons unto glory, to make the captain of their salvation perfect through sufferings.[3]

Christ is our high priest, and He suffered all things like we would and more, so that He would know our grief and our pain, and that He could intercede for us.

If in this life only we have hope in Christ, we are of all men most miserable.[4] If we do not have hope beyond this life, beyond the grave, we are to be most pitied. But, if we are looking to Jesus the Author and Finisher of our faith,[5] knowing we have a hope full of immortality; and if we now taste the powers of the world to come and see the crown that fades not away, then, notwithstanding all our present trials, we are more happy than all men. We live with a joyful confidence, yet at the same time we take delight in the thought of leaving our bodies behind to be at home with the Lord. While we are here, we rejoice in confidence knowing that to be absent from this body is to be present with the Lord.[6]

Therefore, there is Joy in suffering for Christ's sake as it brings sons and daughters into the Kingdom of God. Reaching to the lowest parts of the earth, rolling up our sleeves, and not being afraid to get a little dirt on us, will allow us to reach a lost and dying world for the gospel's sake.

Sometimes it will cost us something to be Christ to those in need. It may require your time, your money, your dignity, but friend - it is worth it to reach that lost soul from the grasp of hell.

---

1. Galatians 5:22-23 KJV
2. Acts 16: 24-33 KJV
3. Hebrews 2:9-10 KJV
4. 1 Corinthians 15:19KJV
5. Hebrews 12:2 KJV
6. Corinthians 5:8 TPT

CHAPTER 12

THE JEWEL OF PERSEVERANCE

Perseverance is a continued effort to do or achieve something despite difficulties, failure or opposition. It is the action or condition; or, an instance of preserving steadfastness, endurance, refusing to give up.

Jesus said in Matthew 24:13: But he that shall endure unto the end, the same shall be saved.[1]

We receive the jewel of perseverance in our reconciliation to Christ. It means in spite of the difficulties we face, we have a reason. We have a hope to offer the world. We have been where others are; we have tried and failed, but God! Yes! He picked us up, held us in His arms of love, showed us His loving mercy, nursed us back to life and helped us begin again.

Now, in-spite of our faults and oppositions, and because we failed the first time around, we refuse to give up. We are like common clay jars that carry this glorious treasure within, so that the extraordinary overflow of power will be seen as God's not ours. Though we experience every kind of pressure we're not crushed. At times we don't even know what to do, but quitting is not an option. We are persecuted by others, but God has not forsaken us. We may be knocked down, but not out.[2]

We are in Gods army and have a determination to see what the end is going to be. The perseverance on the inside of us declares: "The Lord is my shepherd; I shall not want. He makes me to lie down in green pastures: he leadeth me beside the still waters. He restores my soul: he leads me in the paths of righteousness for his name's sake, yea though I walk through the valley of the shadow of death I will fear no evil, for thou art with me, thy rod and thy staff they comfort me. Thou preparest a table before me in the presence of my enemies, thou anointest my head with oil, my cup runs over. Surely goodness and mercy shall follow me all the days of my life and I will dwell in the house of the Lord forever."[3]

You got to have the 'want to' - you have got to have the determination to 'go through!' If you're going to make it through, you got to have the 'want to.'

There is another type of perseverance. It is a 'pressing in,' because we realize we need a touch from Jesus. If we can just press in, from all the noise and the distractions, from all the pulls and struggles that bring distractions, we persevere because God has brought us unto Himself, out of *Lodebar.*

Lodebar, being a place of 'no thing,' and 'no word.' From a place where we had no *word of life,* and basically no life, God brought us into a place of living - from a place of nothing into an inheritance that we cannot even fathom. In today's language, it could be said *Lodebar* was a place in the middle of nowhere. God has brought us from the middle of nowhere to be seated with Him in heavenly places in Christ Jesus.

Just as Jesus called Lazarus out of the grave, He has called you and I out of the grave! We need to put off the grave clothes, embrace the mantle of God, stand up and declare the word of the Lord! Now that you have the Word, speak it over your life; over your family; your friends; your neighborhood; your county; your state; your country; and over the world.

God has brought us out of a place of nothing -no pasture - into His Pasture! We are carrying the Holy Manna, so we need to declare the Word of God as we persevere in this life. Old things have passed away, behold all things have become new.[4]

We must persevere with purpose! Remember, many people were touching Jesus when He asked, *"Who touched me?"*[5] There was one lady that was persevering with purpose, she was pressing in to touch the hem of His garment, because she determined 'if I can just touch the hem of his garment I will be made whole.'[6]

---

1. Matthew 24:13 KJV
2. 2 Corinthians 4:7-9 TPT
3. Psalms 23 KJV
4. 2 Corinthians 5:17 KJV
5. Matthew 9:21 KJV
6. Matthew 9:21 KJV

CHAPTER 13
THE JEWEL OF LOVE

n this reconciliation, God's love is demonstrated to us in such a way that the load we carry is lightened. The weight of sin is heavy, but Jesus said, "Take my yoke upon you, and learn of me; for I am meek and lowly in heart: and ye shall find rest unto your souls. For my yoke is easy and my burden is light."[1] The Passion Translation says, "Simply join your life with mine. Learn my ways and you'll discover that I'm gentle, humble, easy to please. You will find refreshment and rest in me. For all that I require of you will be pleasant and easy to bear."

Have you ever been under the weight of sin so heavy that you did not know which way to turn, or what to do? If you have, I'm sure the same enemy that whispered in my ear when I was at that point in life, has voiced his opinion to you as well! Yet, it's not about an opinion, or the lies of the enemy. What does God's word say? "Come unto me all ye that labor and are heavy laden and I will give you rest."[2] The Word also says we are to be "casting all your care upon Him for He cares for you."[3]

When the weight of sin drops from your life and you feel you could soar on eagle's wings! He teaches us how to lay aside the things that so easily distract us. Sometimes it is one thing at a time, sometimes it is all at once. He is a gentle giant that loves you more than you can imagine. His love is shed a broad in our hearts by the Holy Ghost which is given to us.[4]

Embrace the love Jesus freely gives to us. Not only are we yoked with Jesus, we have a deposit that has been placed on the inside of us.[5] The Holy Spirit is our helper! He goes with us, before us, all around us and behind us. The Holy Spirit will empower us to be a witness and to carry out or walk out our calling. The anointing will be present in your life as you embrace your call and say yes to Jesus. He that loveth not, does not know God for God is love. God puts his love in our heart. [6]

David said, "I am so ashamed. I feel such pain and anguish within me. I can't get away from the sting of my sin against you, Lord! Everything I did, I did right in front of you, for you saw it all. Against you and you above all have I sinned. Everything you saw to me is infallibly true and your judgement conquers me."[7]

David confessed his sin unto the Lord and asked God to forgive him and to cleanse him. "Purify my conscience! Make this leper clean again! Wash me in your love until I am pure in heart. Satisfy me in your sweetness, and my song of joy will return. The places within me you have crushed will rejoice in your healing touch. Hide my sins from your face, erase all my guilt by your saving grace. Create a new, clean heart within me. Fill me with pure thoughts and holy desires, ready to please you. May you never reject me! May you never take from me your sacred Spirit. Let my passion for life be restored, tasting joy in every breakthrough you bring to me. Hold me close to you with a willing spirit that obeys whatever you say. Then I can show to other guilty ones how loving and merciful you are. They will find their way back home to you, knowing that you will forgive them."[8]

You see, your testimony, seasoned with the love of God, will save people from an endless hell. There are people waiting for you to take your rightful place in the kingdom. You were designed to reach them, it is up to you to lead them home! "And others save with fear, pulling them out of the fire; hating even the garment spotted by the flesh."[9]

We should allow the love of God to purify our our heart, as His love permeates our life. He loves you! Because He loves you, because He loves you, because He loves you! That's what He is! **"Love"**

Even if you never return to Him, or respond to Him, He will love you, He can't *not* love you. He wants to demonstrate His love through you.

God desires that we have His love in full operation in our life. Love is the absolute greatest of all gifts. "And if I were to have the gift of prophecy with a profound understanding of Gods hidden secrets, and if I possessed unending supernatural knowledge, and if I had the greatest gift of faith that could move mountains, but have never learned to love, then I am nothing."[10]

We have been given unconditional love from the Father though this reconciliation to bring others into the kingdom. Come on and take your place! The Father is waiting for you.

---

1. Matthew 11: 29-30 KJV
2. Matthew 11:28 KJV
3. 1 Peter 5:7 KJV
4. Romans 5:5 KJV
5. 2 Corinthians 1:22 KJV

6. 1 John 4:8 KJV
7. Psalms 51:1-4 TPT
8. Psalms 51:7-13 TPT
9. Jude 23 KJV
10. 1 Corinthians 13:2 TPT

CHAPTER 14
THE JEWEL OF HOPE

There is another jewel that has been given us through reconciliation. The Jewel of Hope. We have hope in a future, looking to Jesus which is the Author and Finisher of our faith.[1] We hope in the grace God has extended to us as we experience the mercy that He has blessed us with.

If you have ever experienced a situation where you've had to face a judge, knowing that the crime you were guilty of carried a prison sentence, and you were waiting in a jail cell for the sentencing to come, you hoped the judge would have mercy on you. If the judge postponed the trial date and you spent more time in a jail cell, waiting and wondering, hoping to be given a pardon and set free, that 'hope deferred makes the heart sick.'[2] Yet, when the new date arrived, which you hoped for, and the pardon came to pass, it's like a tree of life, like fresh flowing water. "When hope's dream seems to drag on and on, the delay can be depressing. But when at last your dream comes true. Life's sweetness will satisfy your soul. You are called into the hope of your heavenly calling."[3]

"For this is the hope of our salvation. But hope means that we must trust and wait for what is still unseen. For why do we need to hope for something we already have? So, because our hope is set on what is yet unseen, we patiently keep on waiting for its fulfillment. The Holy Spirit takes hold of us in our human frailty to empower us in our weakness, therefore we should not fear failure."[4]

If you never try to succeed at a thing, you never have to worry about failure - but if you are to succeed at anything, there will be failures along the way, so set yourself to fall forward should you fall. The Bible says, "A righteous man falls seven times and rises up again."[5]

We have been justified by His grace and made heirs according to the hope of eternal life.[6] Being justified is just as if you have never sinned. We have been given eternal life. It is a gift! If you accept it, then you will walk out your salvation with fear and trembling[7] in His presence. God will plant inside of you a passion to do what pleases him.

But sanctify the Lord God in your hearts: and be ready to always give an answer to every man that ask you a reason of the hope that is in you with meekness and fear.[8] Sanctification is a daily process; we should walk in sanctification of our heart to God every day, always ready to share with others what God has done for us, able to testify how He has given us the hope of glory. According to 1 John 3:3, all who focus their hope on him will always be purifying themselves, just as Jesus is pure.[9]

We purify our self through the Word of God. As we study God's Word, He reveals Himself to us more and more. Through the revelation we receive, our life begins to transform, lining up with the Word.

Stop imitating the ideals and opinions of the culture around you but be inwardly transformed by the Holy Spirit through a total reformation of how you think. This will empower you to discern God's will as you live a beautiful life, satisfying and perfect in his eyes. Christ gave himself to be crucified for us, that he might redeem us from all iniquity and purify unto himself a peculiar people zealous of good works through the hope of this calling.[10]

---

1. Hebrews 12:12 KJV
2. Proverbs 13:12 KJV
3. Proverbs 13:12 TPT
4. Romans 8:24-25 TPT
5. Proverbs 27:16 KJV
6. Titus 3:7 KJV
7. Philippians 2:12 KJV
8. 1 Peter 3:15 KJV
9. 1 John 3:3 TPT
10. Romans 12:2 TPT

CHAPTER 15

THE JEWEL OF CHARACTER

Character is the eighth jewel in this ring of reconciliation. Therefore if any man be in Christ, he is a new creature: old things have passed away; behold, all things are become new.[1]

Jesus on the inside working on the outside, will bring about change in our life. We put on the character of love and begin to walk a little different; we begin to talk a little different; we may even look different. There is something about having the peace of God in our life that reflects in our countenance. Our moral values change for the better and we see from a much higher perspective.

When Elijah told King Ahab, "Go, eat and drink, for there is the sound of a heavy rain." Ahab went off to eat and drink, but Elijah climbed to the top of Carmel, bent down to the ground, and put his face between his knees. "Go and look toward the sea," he told his servant. And he went up and looked. "There is nothing there," he said. Seven times Elijah said "Go back" the seventh time the servant reported. "A cloud as small as a man's hand is rising from the sea." So, Elijah said, "Go and tell Ahab hitch up your chariot and go down before the rain stops you." Meanwhile, the sky grew black with clouds, the wind rose, a heavy rain came on and Ahab rode off to Jezreel.

Elijah's servant went to look seven times and finally saw a cloud about the size of a man's hand, He saw from a different perspective. That small cloud produced a mighty rain! The more we walk and talk with God the more our character begins to resemble him.

When Moses came down from Mount Sinai with the tablets of the covenant law in his hand, he did not know his face was radiant because he had been in the presence of God. When we spend time in the presence of God, our character changes. Where we might have held onto bitterness, envy, and strife, we choose to let it go, realizing that we have given up our right to hold on to such things. As Christ himself forgave us of our trespasses and sins, so we forgive others who have trespassed against us.[2] We know we have passed from death unto life, because we love the brethren. He that loves not his brother abides in death. Jesus asked, "how can you say you love God whom you have not seen, if you cannot love your brother whom you have seen?"[3]

The character of Jesus begins to shine through us when we accept Christ as our Lord and Savior. We begin to see life itself in a different light. We come to the realization that we war not against flesh and blood, but spiritual wickedness in high places.[4] We take up the understanding that the weapons of our warfare are not carnal but mighty through God to the pulling down of strong holds.[5] Praising God through the good times and the bad, we choose to trust Him through every trial and every circumstance! We refuse to compromise our integrity, even when no one is looking. We remain true to the one that has called us and washed us white as snow. We carry within us the characteristics of Jesus Christ, our Lord and Savior. We have a willingness to forgive because we have been forgiven.

When the prodigal son returned to the Father, he was broken and asked for forgiveness, as a result of realizing his sin. In that moment he had a character makeover. The father rejoiced over his son and threw a party because his son had returned home. This is symbolic of all of heaven rejoicing when a lost person accepts Jesus Christ as their Lord and Savior, or a son or daughter rededicates their life to God.

The jewel of character in the ring of reconciliation sets us apart, we are brought out of darkness into His marvelous light to display His workmanship, to give Him praise and honor. God puts His seal of ownership on us, He has identified us as His own by placing the Holy Spirit in our hearts as the first installment that guarantees everything He has promised us.

---

1. 2 Corinthians 5:17 KJV
2. 1 John 3:4 KJV
3. 1 John 4:20 KJV
4. Ephesians 6:12 KJV
5. 2 Corinthians 10:4 KJV

CHAPTER 16

THE ELDER BROTHER SYNDROME

n Luke chapter 15, Jesus was addressing the once-lost-now-found things. The lost sheep, where he leaves the 99 to find the 1 that is lost leads to the parable of the lost coin where the lady swept the house and searched carefully until she found it. When she found it, she called all of her friends and neighbors together, saying "Rejoice with me! I have found my lost coin!"

In the same way, there is rejoicing in the presence of the angels of God over one sinner who repents. These lead to the parable of the lost Son.

I want us to look at the older brother, now that we know the younger son was a prodigal. He left the father's house, wasted his substance, until finally, when he was at the end of his rope, he came to his senses and returned to the father with a repentant heart.

The older brother was in the field working when he came near to the house. He heard music and rejoicing, so he called one of the servants to himself to inquire what was going on.

"Well, your brother has come home! Your Dad has killed the fatted calf and is throwing a party to celebrate his return." he was told.

This did not set well with the older brother. What was in his heart was about to be revealed.

I want to tell you there are two sons that are lost in this parable. They were both in need of being found. One finds his way back to the Father with a repentant heart.

It is worth noting that the Father never went out looking for the prodigal son (the younger brother), however, he saw him a long way off. Yet in the previous parables what was lost - the sheep and the coin - was being searched for or sought out. I find it interesting that the Father went out and pleaded with the elder son. When the father approached the elder son, what was in his heart came out of his mouth, for out of the abundance of the heart the mouth speaks.[1] A good man brings good things out of the good stored up in his heart, and an evil man brings evil things out of the evil stored up in his heart. For the mouth speaks what the heart is full of.[2]

The older brother was angry and refused to go in and take part of the celebration or partake in his father's joy. Instead, he pointed out to his father, "All these years I have worked for you and never disobeyed your orders, yet you never gave me even a young goat so I could celebrate with my friends. But when this son of yours who has squandered your property with prostitutes come home, you kill the fatted calf for him!"

"My Son," the father said, "you are always with me, and everything I have is yours, but we had to celebrate and be glad, because this brother of yours was dead and is alive again: he was lost and is found."

The older brother was full of pride, jealousy, and bitterness. He resented His father's joy and refused to share in it. He did not come to the father with a repentant heart. Instead he started boasting of his works, and how the father had not recognized what he had done all these years. He was mad because he did not think he was getting all that he deserved for his faithful service. He thought that by obeying the rules, he deserved blessing. God the Father calls us to be doers and not hearers only,[3] but we must realize our salvation is not by works but by His grace. You cannot do enough good or enough service to get into heaven. It is not by works lest any man should boast[4] but by my Spirit says the Lord.

The older brother's motive was to receive, not to show love to the father. He did not care about the father any more than the younger brother had when he demanded his inheritance while his father was still alive. Maybe the real reason the elder brother was angry was because his younger brother had squandered half of their shared inheritance. Now that he witnessed the younger being welcomed back in the family, he knew they would both receive a slice from a much smaller piece of pie when the father died.

Our relationship with God must be centered on pleasing him, loving him, and always growing closer to him. The love of God must be our starting point, our motives must be pure, we need to love God for who he is, not for what he can give us.

The older thought his younger brother's sinfulness was unforgivable. He was angry that "this son of yours, who has squandered your property with prostitutes" was the object of his father's affection and celebration. An attitude of unforgiveness arose in his heart - his father might be willing to forgive, but by golly he wouldn't! His standards were higher than his father's.

Do you know anyone that thinks their standards are higher than the Father's? Anyone that will throw your past sins in your face when God has forgiven you demonstrate such high standards.

This sin was unforgivable in the elder brother's eyes. While the younger brother might be his father's son, he was no longer a brother to him.

How arrogant and prideful! It was not his place to judge or hold his brothers past sins against him. Christians do this all the time, identifying people by their past, holding on to 'the dirt' in someone's history, so they can bring it up again later.

If the father who was wronged can forgive, why can't we forgive? He was lost and did not know it.

Jesus was telling these parables in the presence of tax collectors and sinners that were gathering around to hear Jesus, but the Pharisees and the teachers of the law muttered, "This man welcomes sinners and eats with them."

As Jesus told these parables it was spilling over into the ears of the Pharisees. As he was talking about the prodigal son, I'm sure they were thinking, 'this son doesn't deserve to even be part of the family anymore!'

I think Jesus brought out the elder brother's actions to show that pride and arrogance is not pleasing to the Father. This elder brother was no different than Pharisee in Luke 18: The Pharisee stood by himself and prayed; "God, I thank you that I am not like other people, robbers, evildoers, adulterers, or even like this tax collector!" [5]They had a form of godliness but denied the power of God.

God has not called us to walk with Him in a powerless form. He sent us Holy Spirit to walk out our call with power and with anointing. Our salvation is free, but the anointing will cost you, it means that we die to self, we lay down our life, take up our cross and follow Him. The enemy of our soul tries to stand between us and our destiny, but God sees us as his finished product, doing what He has called us to do. You may have failed God - in fact we have all failed God - but that does not make us a failure! You may have lied but that does not make you a liar. You may have stolen but that does not make you a thief!

Come on! Declare what God has spoken over you, do not agree or make a pact with the devil. You are an overcomer! Greater is He that is in you than he that is in the world. This is the season for the prodigals to come home, God is throwing a party and you are called to be the main event! So, pray this prayer with me and return to the Father.

Heavenly Father, I have sinned against you, and I ask you to forgive me of my sins. I pray you would cleanse me from all unrighteousness, Jesus I confess with my mouth, and I believe in my heart you died on the cross and rose again the third day. I pray that you would help me forgive myself for my past sin, as you have forgiven me. I put it under the blood and declare myself free. Create in me a clean heart and renew a right Spirit in me. In the name of Jesus, I pray.

Amen.

---

1. Luke 6:45 NIV
2. Luke 15:28-32 NIV
3. James 1:22 KJV
4. Ephesians 2:9 KJV
5. Luke 18:11 NIV

CHAPTER 17
THE SHOES

find it amazing that the father of the prodigal son instructed his servants to bring shoes for his feet, along with the robe and the ring. This denotes the fathers concern for his sons well being and meaning for life. In those days they walked everywhere they went. To be concerned for his feet was love in demonstration. The shoes would be an asset in fulfilling his renewed purpose. Apparently when this young man returned home, he was barefoot (without purpose). He had not given much or any thought of preparation for his future, however, the father insisted upon making those preparations that set his son apart from the servants. Not only for the servants to give honor and respect to his son, but anyone that encountered him to know he was restored to sonship.

I believe the shoes (sandals) represented renewed purpose. This son had returned home, the father said, "he was dead and is alive again." His father was eager to restore him to sonship to carry out his purpose in the family. Restoration of purpose, there is no doubt that in the four gifts the father bestowed upon his son, that the idea of becoming a hired servant in his fathers' house was abolished in his mind forever. He was accepted by his father, welcomed with open arms, accepted in the beloved.

He was given the best robe. This was a sign of forgiveness, a covering of sin and shame through love and grace. The father demonstrated that he had no intention of exposing his sin, his faults or failures. This is so much like Father God. He gave us Jesus, the best heaven had to redeem us and provide a covering for our sins, our faults and failures. He doesn't tell us we have to do penance for our sins, before we come to Him, He said come as you are. Just like this prodigal that could not change his condition on his own, his best recourse was to come to the father just as he was, the same applies to you and me. We can't change our sinful nature on our own, however, we can come just as we are. Hebrews 4:16 says Let us therefore come boldly unto the throne of grace, that we may obtain mercy, and find grace to help in time of trouble.[1]

The ring restored his identity, his sonship, and his belonging to the family. His value and his authority. It was somewhat of a signet ring that allowed him to operate in the authority of the father. Jesus gave us his authority to use as kingdom representatives over all the power of the enemy.

The shoes gave him renewed purpose and meaning for life, (hope). Without hope we would be of all men most miserable. This young mans honor had been restored, he could now operate in his father's affairs. He rejoined the family as a son with authority and renewed purpose. He could now learn the father's heart and walkout his purpose in the love of his father, knowing his authority under the father was approved.

Now a celebration was being prepared, the father said, "my son who was dead is now alive again, he was lost and is now found." They began to be merry and make music and maybe some dancing, the celebration was on. The father had instructed the servants to kill the fatted calf, one that had been stall fed for a season and was ready to be processed and cooked. He said, "Let us eat and be merry, its celebration time!"

The father was so excited that his son had returned home unharmed, it did not matter where he had been, what he had done or even why he had returned home. The father was rejoicing because his son was home. His very presence told the father everything he needed to know.

Now the elder brother heard the commotion and inquired as to what was going on. He was told, your brother has come home, and your father has killed the fatted calf to celebrate his return. The elder brother was angry and full of accusations, he had no understanding of his father's heart. In fact, I would say, "even though he had remained at home and served the father all this time, he did not know his father". He was more concerned with works than just being his father's son and pleasing his father.

Notice the father never accused his son of his past, but the elder brother accused him of things he speculated he had done. The only way I know to say this is the elder was being a spokesman for Satan. You may say, that's pretty bold buddy, is it? The scripture says Satan is the accuser of the brethren.[2] Here we have the elder brother accusing the younger brother. The father never even brought up the path the young man took upon leaving home, he was just overjoyed his son had returned home.

Jesus said He would leave the ninety-nine to go after the one sheep that had gone astray, meaning, He cares about what concerns us. If we have fallen by the wayside the father longs to restore us.

Sometimes, those that feel they have not failed God or walked away from him, often gossip about those that have, often in the form of accusations. We should pray for our brothers and sisters that have been tripped up by the enemy and be willing to reach out to them in an effort to restore them back to the faith. We should realize there is no big sin verses a little sin, In Fathers eyes sin is sin! We have all come short of the Glory of God.[3]

The father of the prodigal son went to great lengths to cover his son and re-establish him to his rightful place as a son in the house.

First, he took the shame and reproach upon himself, when he lifted his tunic and ran to meet his son, probably to get to him before he entered the village. In the Jewish culture it was humiliating and shameful for a man to show his bare legs, therefore, it was considered a disgrace for a man wearing a tunic to run, nevertheless this is what the father done. He knew, 'if I can get to my son before the community gets to him, I can restore him to sonship, and everyone will have to honor my decision.'

In that day, if a Jewish son lost his inheritance among Gentiles and returned home the community would call a meeting and perform a ceremony called the "kezazah" meaning "a severing of connections, a cutting off". They would break a large pot in front of him and yell "You are now cutoff from your people!" The community would then totally reject him and treat him as an outcast among his fellow Jews. When the father ran to his son and took his reproach upon himself, dressed in in the best robe, put a ring on his finger and shoes on his feet, welcomed him home with a loving celebration reunion it was clear - there would be no need for the kezazah ceremony to take place.

This is much like us when we separate our self from the Father. Satan is like a roaring lion seeking whom he may devour.[4] He tries to set us up for the kill, but thank God he doesn't have the final say, Father does!

When we come to Papa (Abba) with a repentant heart, He forgives. What He forgives, He forgets, causing those that are set free to be free indeed.[5]

Even when our elder brother does not understand or accept the restoration of a prodigal, when the father does the work, it is finished. Celebration will go on with or without elder brothers' approval.

The elder brothers attitude resembled that of a religious spirit that slips its way in among the brethren. The same religious spirit that crucified Christ. We are not the judge or the jury, so we need to leave that in Fathers hands. It is our duty to love one another and be our brother's keeper. If one is overtaken in a fault we are to try and restore that person, not shun them, despise them, talk about them and cast them out of the house of God.

Ephesians chapter 5 speaks of the armor we as children of God are to put on, verse 15 in the Passion Translation says, "Stand on your feet alert, then you'll always be ready to share the blessings of peace." Spread the good news wherever you go, someone is always eager to hear the gospel.

The steps of a good man are ordered by the Lord: And he delighteth in his way.[6] The Father has ordered (ordained) our steps and He takes delight as we go along the path He has laid out before us. Your mistake, failure, nor fault caught God by surprise, He already knew what you would do and how you would react. He has a plan for your life.

For I know the thoughts that I think toward you, saith the Lord, thoughts of peace and not evil to give you an expected end. [7]

Therefore, let us shod our feet with the preparation of the gospel of peace.[8] The shoes prepare us, as ambassadors with a stance of readiness to be about the Fathers business (kingdom business).

Join in the celebration, we are to rejoice over one soul repenting, It's not our place to stand in judgement of a fallen warrior, in fact we are to help our fallen warriors arise.

The fruit of the righteous is a tree of life; and He that winneth souls is wise.[9]

---

1. KJV
2. Revelation 12:10 KJV
3. Romans 3:23 KJV
4. 1 Peter 5:8 KJV
5. John 8:36 KJV
6. Psalms 37:23 KJV
7. Jeremiah 29:11 KJV
8. Ephesians 5:15-16 KLV
9. Proverbs 11:30 KJV

ABOUT THE AUTHOR

Dwayne Jacobs is a lover of God the Father, Jesus and Holy Spirit. He exists to encourage and motivate others to praise and worship God in Spirit and in Truth. Dwayne is devoted to his family and has a heart to reach the fatherless and express the Father's love to them.

Dwayne was raised in a single parent home by his mother Doris C. Jacobs in a rural community in North Carolina. One of his fond memories growing up was a period of time before his Mom owned a car. She would get home from work, fix dinner, then walk a mile in one direction to share the gospel and pray for people that would be gathered at the local boot-leggers home. She would then return home, Dwayne at her side the entire way.

Doris taught Dwayne and his brother to work, to love the Lord, and to walk by faith. The family planted a garden every year. At harvest time, after processing the food they had raised, Doris and her children would take a good portion of the food they had processed to neighbors that were in need. They did so as the Lord would lead. In this way, she taught her sons the importance of hearing and obeying the voice of the Lord, as well as what it means to serve others in need.

As an Evangelist, Dwayne serves a one hundred mile radius of his community as an Industrial Salesman, sharing the gospel one on one. He exemplifies Christ in the market-place, preaching everywhere he goes, using words when necessary.

Dwayne and his beautiful wife have six children and one adopted son and are partners of New Life Christian Church in Augusta, Ga.

The Destiny Series Books

STRATEGIC TRAINING TO DISCOVER YOU

THE DESTINY SERIES
IDENTITY
REBECCA D. BENNETT

THE DESTINY SERIES
PURPOSE
REBECCA D. BENNETT

THE DESTINY SERIES
AUTHORITY
REBECCA D. BENNETT

THE DESTINY SERIES
LEGACY
REBECCA D. BENNETT

The Destiny Series is designed to help you discover the who and the why that you are. You are designed to become a great leader that God intended you to be, and you can reach your maximum potential in the ministry that the Lord Jesus gave every person (Matthew 28:19).

This dynamic and interactive series is available for individual or group study, as well as an author led course. To learn more, use QR code to view books now available by Author, Rebecca D. Bennett and much more.

Education

MAKING EXCELLENCE VISIBLE

KLI GULF COAST

Kingdom Leadership Institute Gulf Coast

The leadership institute of choice prepares you for leadership in the Kingdom of God. The strategy of Kingdom Leadership Institute Gulf Coast is individualized. Your leadership training can begin at any level of spiritual and ministry maturity. We start where you are with what you do.

As one can function in any aspect of culture, once taught to function in kingdom culture, the Institute educates and prepares students for any arena of occupation. We honor kingdom leaders from every walk of life. Students come from many professions and occupations.

Partnered with KLI Jacksonville, our course intensives develop mature individuals to impact the current culture with Kingdom culture. Determine today to engage your life's work at the starting gate of Kingdom Leadership Institute Gulf Coast. For more information or to enroll, please use QR code or contact us via email at kligulfcoast@gmail.com.

Serve, Train, Empower
We Bring the Trainer to You.

- Community Advancement
- Business Training
- Leadership Development

Wells of SouthGate is a training, equipping, and activating center on the Mississippi Gulf Coast.

Our passion is to see each person matured to fulfill our God-given dreams and destiny, to become a flourishing, contributing member of their society. For more information, use QR code to visit the Wells of SouthGate website.

A Publishing Assist Company
Honor & Excellence as the seedbed of your written work

3Trees Publishing was born the result of the architectural build out of Wells of SouthGate. Following the blueprints for the region, 3Trees Publishing serves to reconnect creatives with their kingdom calling by supplying a framework of excellence for all printed work. This endeavor reintroduces and reconstitutes the original intent and design for the Spanish West Florida Territory and beyond.

Let the expression of your purpose be revealed as you prepare legacy for those who come after. For more information, use QR code to contact 3Trees.

THE NAME Speaks by Angela Broussard
His sound reverberates. Can you hear Him speak your name?

It is said that life is a journey and we are pilgrims on it. Discovering our strengths, weaknesses and opponents on the journey exposes the reality of the spiritual realm - and just how fortified it is. Each installment of Doors, Gates, and Thresholds will equip you to successfully navigate the unseen structural components of both the Kingdom of God and the Kingdom of darkness, leading you to victory upon victory. This, in turn, will empower the corporate expression of the Ekklesia, releasing power in greater measure, and you bring your victory to bear upon the whole.

The Name Speaks is the introduction to the Master Poet and His creation: you. Engage in the formation of your identity within the large context of the Kingdom, and come to know your vital role in service to the King. To learn more, use QR code to see books and tools by & to contact Author, Angela Broussard.

Designs x Laura
Let's manifest your vision

Designs x Laura is a brand and service for helping others find and interpret their vision. Whether you offer a product or service, are new or established in your field or maybe don't know what the next step is for you, you're covered!

For web design, graphic design and marketing services, please use QR code to view our portfolio, contact information or get started and book your consultation! If you don't see a specific need listed, feel free to reach out and our team will be happy to assist and discuss the innovation of your ideas.